VIVA LAS BUFFY!

PAUL LEE *and* BRIAN HORTON

VIVA LAS BUFFY!

based on the television series created by
JOSS WHEDON

writers **SCOTT LOBDELL & FABIAN NICIEZA**

penciller **CLIFF RICHARDS**

inker **WILL CONRAD**

colorists **DAVE McCAIG & LISA GONZALES**

letterer **CLEM ROBINS**

cover art **PAUL LEE & BRIAN HORTON**

This story takes place before Buffy the Vampire Slayer's first season.

titan books

publisher
MIKE RICHARDSON

editor
SCOTT ALLIE
with MATT DRYER

designer
LANI SCHREIBSTEIN

art director
MARK COX

special thanks to
DEBBIE OLSHAN AT FOX LICENSING
AND DAVID CAMPITI AT GLASS HOUSE GRAPHICS

PUBLISHED BY
TITAN BOOKS,
A DIVISION OF TITAN PUBLISHING GROUP PLC
144 SOUTHWARK STREET
LONDON
SE1 0UP

FIRST EDITION
JULY 2003
ISBN: 1 - 84023 - 643 - 4

1 3 5 7 9 10 8 6 4 2

PRINTED IN ITALY

INTRODUCTION

Los Angeles high school freshman Buffy Summers shouldered an overwhelming burden, what with worrying about boys, cheerleading, and coordinating shoes, who could deal?

Then a mysterious man named Merrick came to her. Told her he was a Watcher. Said she was the Chosen One. Called her The Slayer, humanity's protector from the forces of darkness.

"Yeah, right," she thought. Then she encountered her first vampire. And her second. And a lot more. As Buffy began to train for her destiny, a vampiric overlord named Lothos infiltrated the underground of Los Angeles. With the help of a high school slacker named Pike, Buffy stopped Lothos, but at the cost of Merrick's life, her high school social status, and her criminal record.

Because the gymnasium burned down during the vampire attack, Buffy has been suspended from school pending expulsion hearings. Her parents are having marital problems. And she's a fifteen-year-old Slayer without a Watcher.

The end of the original motion picture was just the beginning of her story...

PAUL LEE *and* BRIAN HORTON

DON'T BOTHER.

YES...YOU WILL!

ALL THAT DOES IS SWISS CHEESE OUR CLOTHES...

...AND PISS US OFF!

CAKOW BAKOW

Y'KNOW, COPS NEVER LISTEN...

YEAH, NOW LOOK AT THE HOLE--

FWP

--IN MY SHIRT--?

HERE'S SOME INFORMATION ON PRIVATE SCHOOLS.

JOYCE...I JUST DON'T KNOW IF WE CAN AFFORD IT RIGHT NOW...

BUFFY HAD ASKED ME WHAT IT HAD BEEN LIKE-- WATCHING MY PARENTS GET *DIVORCED.*

I SHRUGGED MY SHOULDERS, SAID, "I DON'T KNOW."

SHE WANTED TO BLAME HERSELF. BLAME THE WHOLE SLAYER THING.

BUT DEEP DOWN SHE KNEW THE PROBLEMS HAD BEEN THERE FOR A WHILE.

SHE WANTED MY SUPPORT. I GAVE HER, "I DON'T KNOW."

I'M A SET OF *WHEELS* TO HER. AND WHEN SHE ASKS FOR MORE, I'M A *FLAT TIRE.*

MY ENTIRE LIFE, I *NEVER* CARED ABOUT ANYONE ELSE, AND WHEN I FINALLY DO...

--PETITION TO READMIT THE STUDENT TO *HEMERY HIGH SCHOOL* IS HEREBY *DENIED.*

BUT--

BUT--

EXPELLED.

THAT'LL LOOK GOOD ON YOUR COLLEGE APPLICATIONS, BUFFY.

OH NO, WAIT--I FORGOT --YOU CAN'T GO TO COLLEGE NOW!

NO, *JOYCE*-- THIS NEW, CALM THING WORKS FOR YOU, BUT I'M *MAD!*

HANK, PLEASE...

LOOK AT THE MESS SHE'S MADE!

TAKE FRESHMAN YEAR OVER AGAIN AT A NEW SCHOOL? I HEARD.

IT'S JUST FOR THE REST OF THIS YEAR, DAD. I CAN--

WHAT ABOUT BETWEEN NOW AND THEN, BUFFY?

IF YOU HAVEN'T NOTICED, I *WORK* FOR A LIVING--

AND YOUR MOTHER HAS HER-- WHATEVER SHE HAS-- WE CAN'T WATCH YOU ALL DAY LONG!

"WHO'S GOING TO KEEP AN EYE ON YOU NOW?"

A SPECIAL MEETING OF THE *WATCHER'S COUNCIL* HAS BEEN CALLED TO ORDER.

OUTSIDE OF LONDON...

MMFFF

HEY, WATCH WHERE YOU'RE--

--UHM... NEVER MIND.

LOTS OF NEWBIES COMING IN FROM VEGAS.

WE'RE--UHM--JUST TRYING TO SPREAD THE WORD.

AND WHAT WORD WOULD THAT BE?

OUR KIND'S ALWAYS WELCOME AT THE GOLDEN TOUCH CASINO!

I LIKE AN OPEN INVITATION...

CAN'T SAVE THE WORLD UNTIL YOU GET YOUR *DRIVER'S LICENSE*.

NO WAY.

BRIGHT LIGHTS.

NO.

SHOWGIRLS.

NO.

WE'LL PROBABLY HAVE TO *SHARE* A TACKY MOTEL ROOM FOR DAYS.

OKAY.

I KNOW IT'S JUST AN *EXCUSE* FOR HER TO RUN AWAY.

USE ONE SET OF RESPONSIBILITIES TO AVOID ANOTHER.

BUT I DON'T SAY THAT TO HER.

I DON'T SAY ANYTHING.

ONE WEEK IN VEGAS.

I'M SHACKING UP WITH A RUNAWAY WHO ALSO HAPPENS TO BE THE *SLAYER*.

AND WE'RE LOOKING FOR A *VAMPIRE FACTORY*.

AND FOR THE *NINETIETH* TIME IN THE LAST TEN SECONDS, I'M THINKING, WHAT IN THE NAME OF *JERRY FALWELL* AM I DOING HERE!

EMPLOYEE EN ONLY

I GOT A JOB AS A *VALET* AT THE *GOLDEN TOUCH*. GOOD WAY TO SEE THE COMINGS AND GOINGS.

BUFFY WILL COVER STUFF *INSIDE* THE CASINO.

SO--uhm... GOOD LUCK.

YOU TOO. IF YOU SEE ANYTHING-- YOU KNOW, *FANGY*--

--I'LL SCREAM VERY LOUD.

OKAY.

OKAY.

SHE'S RUNNING AWAY, BUT WHAT ABOUT *ME*? I WANT TO THINK MAYBE RUNNING TO SOMETHING...BUT *WHAT*?

I DON'T PAY YOU TO STAND AROUND, KID.

HAPPILY EVER AFTER? I GOT AS MUCH A SHOT AS *THAT GUY* DOES...

BREAKING BONES I UNDERSTAND, SENDS A MESSAGE, BUT *BLOODLETTING* SEEMS...

MEDIEVAL, RIGHT? I'M NOT A FAN MYSELF, BUT THE OWNERS HAVE THEIR WAYS.

DO I GET TO MEET THE *OWNERS?*

YOU DON'T WANT TO, YOU MEET THEM, MEANS YOU SCREWED UP.

GO GET AN ICE CREAM, KID. I GOT PERSONAL BUSINESS NOW.

"PLEASE--HE DOESN'T HAVE TO KNOW!"

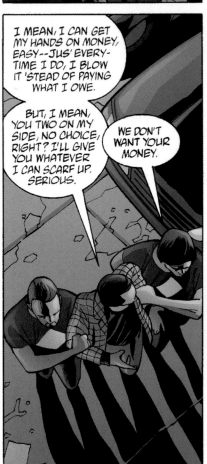

I MEAN, I CAN GET MY HANDS ON MONEY, EASY--JUS' EVERY-TIME I DO, I BLOW IT 'STEAD OF PAYING WHAT I OWE.

BUT, I MEAN, YOU TWO ON MY SIDE, NO CHOICE, RIGHT? I'LL GIVE YOU WHATEVER I CAN SCARF UP. SERIOUS.

WE DON'T WANT YOUR MONEY.

OH GOD...

AAAAAAH

I COULDN'T HAVE SAVED HIM. COULD I?

HOW FAR AM I SUPPOSED TO GO WITH THIS?

I MEAN, SHOULD THIS BE A JOB FOR A *NORMAL* PERSON?

AND CALLING *MYSELF* NORMAL JUST SHOWS YOU *HOW* ABNORMAL ALL THIS IS *!*

I GOTTA GET BUFFY...

OOOMPH.

MY LAST WORDS: OOOMPH. GREAT. CLOD. HEY NOW...

SNAPT

TERROR-INSPIRED BRAIN CELLS. PIKE IS EN FUEGO.

OF COURSE IT IS. WHAT WITH YOU AND MR. BRYARDALE IN SUCH HEATED COMPETITION AND ALL.

IT IS A COMPETITION TO EVERYONE ELSE *BUT* ME.

WELL MR. GILES, SHOULD YOU HAVE INTEREST IN *ADDITIONAL* RESEARCH -- OF A *ROUTINE* NATURE, OF COURSE...

HMPH. NICE TO STILL SEE A BIT OF THE *RIPPER* BENEATH THE *TWEED*...

YOU ARE CERTAIN OF THIS, *MR. WYNDHAM-PRICE?*

ABSOLUTELY, SIR. MR. GILES INTENDS TO DABBLE IN *FORBIDDEN MAGICKS.*

WELL, WE'LL SEE ABOUT THAT...

MICK JONES SAID IT. *STAY OR GO?*

I COULD GO. WOULD THAT LEAVE BUFFY IN *TROUBLE?*

AND IF I STAY? DOUBLE-TROUBLE.

SO COME ON AND LET ME KNOW.

HUH?

WHAT?

YOU READ MINDS?

NOT THAT I KNOW OF. WHY?

NOTHING. COINCIDENCE.

I KNOW YOU'RE *SCARED*, PIKE. I WOULD BE, TOO--

--IF I STOPPED TO THINK ABOUT IT FOR FIVE SECONDS--

--WHICH I CAN'T DO, BECAUSE IF I DID...

...THEN YOU'D BE TOO SCARED TO FIGHT.

AND THAT MIGHT LEAD TO VERY *DEAD.*

AND THAT'S WHAT I'M AFRAID OF.

YOU DYING?

NO, YOU DYING.

WELL, THAT'S SOMETHING ELSE I DON'T THINK ABOUT, 'CAUSE, YOU KNOW...

OH.

UHM... MAYBE YOU SHOULD START...

TERM'S "CONJOINED TWINS." I LOVE THE LOOK ON PEOPLE'S FACES...

HOWDY, MEAT, I'M MARCUS SIDLE. THIS IS MY SISTER, MARY LOU. YOU ASKIN' HOW COME HE IS AN' SHE'S NOT?

"LONG STORY, SHORT...

"OUR GRAND-DADDY, GARNER SIDLE, STARTED A GAMBLIN' DEN MORE'N SEVENTY YEARS AGO--FIRST ONE UP, BEFORE BUGSY SIEGEL CAME INTO TOWN.

"HE GOT BIT BY A VAMP 'ROUND 1930, BUT KEPT RUNNIN' THE PLACE.

"AFTER DADDY GREW UP, HE RAN THE PLACE BY DAY--TURNED DEBTORS INTO FOOD FOR GRAMPS--PLACE GREW, VAMPS LIKED IT HERE--

"--GRANDPA SORTA GOT VAMPIRE ALZHEIMERS AN' HE TURNED ME--BUT MARY LOU STAKED HIM 'FORE HE COULD NIP HER.

"WE'RE KINDA STUCK LIKE THIS NOW--NO PUN INTENDED."

NOT THE MOST FUNCTIONAL O' FAMILIES, I'LL GIVE Y'ALL THAT MUCH...

"...BUT NAME ME ONE FAMILY THAT IS NORMAL?"

--BUT WHAT CAN WE DO?

THE POLICE SAID HER FRIEND PIKE IS MISSING, TOO--

--THEY RAN AWAY SOMEWHERE-- WE DON'T KNOW WHERE--

LOS ANGELES. THE SUMMERS RESIDENCE.

DON'T YOU EVEN CARE, HANK?

OF COURSE I DO, JOYCE--

--SO AM I SUPPOSED TO STOP WORKING? DRIVE ALL OVER CALIFORNIA CALLING OUT HER NAME?

BUT SHE'S ONLY FIFTEEN!

--SHE CAN'T DEAL WITH ALL THE HORRIBLE THINGS THAT ARE OUT THERE!

SHE BURNED THE SCHOOL GYM DOWN, JOYCE!

WE HAVE NO IDEA WHAT SHE'D BEEN DOING BEFORE SHE RAN AWAY.

BUFFY'S DIARY

"I MEAN, WHO CAN BE EXPECTED TO KNOW WHAT THEIR KIDS ARE UP TO TWENTY-FOUR HOURS A DAY?"

THE *WATCHER'S COUNCIL* OUTSIDE OF *LONDON*...

THE ALLEGATIONS RAISED AGAINST YOU ARE SERIOUS.

I CAN'T TELL YOU HOW DISAPPOINTED I AM WITH YOU, *MR. GILES*.

I UNDER-STAND, *QUENTIN*, BUT IF I MAY...

DENY THE CHARGES?

HAVE YOU ENGAGED IN RITUALS INVOLVING *BLACK MAGICKS*--

--TO ELIMINATE *WILLEM BRYARDALE* AS YOUR COMPETITION FOR THE POSITION OF *WATCHER*?

I DO INDEED, DENY IT--QUITE *VEHEMENTLY*.

I CAN PROVE IT TO YOU, BUT WE MUST GO TO *BRYARDALE'S* DORMITORY...

WE'RE HERE. I SEE NOTHING UNTOWARD.

BACK AWAY A BIT...

EGRAJIA VANAHALLA PERMUSERA PERMUSERREE!

OH.

I USED *BLACK ARTS* ONLY AS A MEANS TO EXPOSE BRYARDALE'S ACTIVITIES!

QUITE THE *IRONIC CONUNDRUM,* ISN'T IT, RUPERT?

...I'M NOT GONNA BE AN ANCHOR ANYMORE!

WHAT ARE YOU--

TRYING TO SAVE US!

OKAY, THAT WAS VERY *TESTOSTERONY,* BUT IT ONLY LEFT US ONE WAY OUT...

NOT SMART.

PUFFED-UP MANLY MAN LASTED ALL OF TWO SECONDS.

UP!

BUT-- WHOA--

OW.

IS THERE A *FIRE* STAIRWELL?

OF COURSE THERE IS! THE GOLDEN TOUCH CONFORMS T' THE FIRE CODE!

UNFORTUNATELY FOR THE TWO OF YOU...

...WE SENT OUR BOYS THROUGH IT!

GET BEHIND ME, PIKE.

BACK TO SQUARE ONE. TRAPPED.

AND WHY DO I GET THE FEELING THE ONLY SOLUTION TO THE PROBLEM...

OR AT THE VERY LEAST, *ESCAPE.*

BUT SHE'S GOTTA WORRY ABOUT FIGHTING THEM AND PROTECTING ME.

AGAIN.

THE NUMBERS DON'T ADD UP.

THE SLAYER CAN'T BE WORRIED ABOUT HER *FRIENDS* OR HER *FAMILY.*

NOT IF SHE WANTS TO SURVIVE FOR VERY LONG.

SO NO MATTER WHICH WAY I LOOK AT THIS THING...

...I KEEP COMING UP WITH ONLY ONE SIMPLE WAY TO SOLVE THE PROBLEM.

...BUT HELPING BUFFY IS MORE IMPORTANT THAN ANYTHING...

FOR HOW MUCH LONGER?

I MEAN...HOW MUCH LONGER DOES THIS INSANITY CONTINUE BEFORE IT'S ALL OVER?

BEFORE I DIE OR SHE DIES?

A WEEK? A MONTH? A YEAR, TOPS.

BUFFY--STOP--WAIT FOR A MINUTE!

WHAT'S YOUR PLAN?

PLAN? STAKE. ASH. PLAN.

THAT'S A HOTEL FILLED WITH VAMPIRES. YOU'RE GOING TO KILL ALL OF THEM BEFORE THEY KILL YOU?

YOU HAVE A BETTER SUGGESTION?

YES, I DO!

WE GET ON MY MOTORCYCLE AND GET THE HELL OUT OF HERE!

WE LIVE NORMAL LIVES-- NO VAMPIRES, NO SLAYING--

BUT YOU STILL KEEP THAT OUTFIT...

YOU TRIED TO KILL YOURSELF.

I THOUGHT YOU WOULD DIE TRYING TO PROTECT ME.

I TORE THROUGH ALL OF THEM.

ONLY BECAUSE YOU DIDN'T HAVE TO WORRY ABOUT ME!

YOU CAN'T HAVE *FRIENDS* ...YOU CAN'T LOVE ME...NOT IF YOU'RE GONNA BE THE SLAYER.

I CAN'T HELP IT, PIKE. I THINK...IT'S WHO I *HAVE* TO BE--WHO I *AM*.

I KNOW. AND I--I *LOVE* YOU TOO MUCH TO SEE YOU DIE BECAUSE OF ME.

NO--IT DOESN'T HAVE TO BE THIS WAY--

BUT IT *IS*.

BE GOOD. GET THEM BEFORE THEY GET YOU.

"UNTIL DEATH DO YOU PART." THEY MAKE YOU BELIEVE IT'S *FOREVER*.

MAYBE THIS LOVE WILL LAST FOREVER, AT LEAST FOR *ME*, I THINK.

STUPID ME.

THE THINGS PEOPLE DO FOR LOVE...

END

GET THE OFFICIAL
BUFFY MAGAZINE!

FREE VALENTINE'S CARD!

FREE POSTER! NEW EPISODES REVIEWED!

Buffy the vampire slayer™

CHASING AMY

Elizabeth Anne Allen on her return to *Buffy*

DECONSTRUCTING ANYA

Issue 44
Mar 2003
£2.95
(Cover 1 of 2)

Exclusive set report on origin episode!

SUNNYDALE NEWS The latest on *Buffy* Season Seven, plus *Angel* Season Four

ON SALE AT ALL GOOD NEWSAGENTS!
CALL 01536 764 646 TO SUBSCRIBE

GRAPHIC NOVEL STAKE OUT!

Buffy THE VAMPIRE SLAYER

Note from the Underground

Buffy THE VAMPIRE SLAYER

Willow & Tara

ALL NEW, BUFFY Adventures From Titan Books

Available from all good bookshops, or telephone
Titan Mail Order on 01536 76 46 46.
(Office hours open Monday – Friday 9am-5pm.)